Stories Of Others
San Clemente

Roger Cerny

ISBN-10: 1688791272
ISBN-13: 978-1688791275

First Edition, Part 1 revision

Song lyric from "Hey, Hey, My, My (Into the Black)" by Neil Young, Crazy Horse

All photographs by Roger Cerny

For more information, please visit:
IG: stories_of_others_the_book
Facebook: Roger Cerny
For press or other inquiries contact: KLC Management Ink.
StoriesOfOthers@yahoo.com

For Eillo, because if it wasn't for her
being brought into my life, these stories
might have not been made

Stories of Others
San Clemente

Part 1

Today is Thursday. I just got back from a trip to San Clemente, where I left last Tuesday. I've been in, through and around San Clemente but nothing like this last trip…

I was at my favorite spot for a little bit of time that morning. While tending to business a motorhome backs in right next to me. Their stereo was cranking, my quiet time came to an end. I would have moved but my battery was dead. My option was clear, I'm going to have to ask these intruders for a jumpstart. What I didn't know was a new adventure was getting ready to start.

The first evening, I was parked on the bluff. I was putting things away and a person walked up to me and said that his name is Craig and you might know who I am, or maybe who my friends are. I'm lonely and sleep in the caves down below in the bluffs. I said ohhh... I couldn't stop what I was doing and ask Craig how he was but he went on to tell me his story. Craig, a total stranger to me, told me that his wife just died recently. Craig went on for a while telling me how he is a well-known surfboard glasser. I just listened. He had been drinking for awhile, I was reminded of my own drinking style.

My drinking has been a lifelong battle. It started when I turned 13 years old and it continues to be an ongoing fight. Craig was telling me how he was not a drunk before. It is just now that his wife took her own life. Craig is having a hard and lonely time with it. Plus the death only occurred a few months ago. It's pretty harsh but I told him he has to get past the grief. Honestly I have no idea why I told him that so I apologized. Still can't figure why I would tell somebody that while he is still missing his wife.

The only thing I can figure is that it would resonate in Craig's mind as a reminder to push into the pain of missing his dead wife and how he could get control of his life. It was a strange feeling, for me to be so direct, but that is what I told Craig. He just nodded and said he has heard the same from other peers. I tried to encourage him as much as my energy would permit. I just wasn't really sure how to handle this situation. Craig was a very nice guy. He was telling me that he's been talking to the pastor at the Keystone Church.

The pastor was inviting Craig to go to a place called The Ranch out in the desert. That is what he kept repeating so I could tell it was on his mind. Kinda hard to tell though since he had been drinking. What was obvious is he was not denying the fact that he was using alcohol to cope with the pain. I asked him if he had a Bible. He said he did but the tide washed it out to sea. I gave him a Gospel of John and a New Testament. I gave him one with large print saying that it might be easier to read under the dim light. Craig started reading it and immediately I was surprised to see the sudden interest. I pointed out John 10:10 and talked about how the devil comes to destroy us. I told Craig about how sheep hear the Shepherd's voice. It seemed to penetrate through the blur of alcohol and I could sense a little hope from Craig.

I feel that I learn from others when I let them tell me their story. I feel like the mission I am on is as a seed-planting missionary, that's all, just being there with a Bible in hand and offering a person to make a decision, while working close to my home, my roots, where I used to play, explore, and dream. Sometimes it is uncomfortable to be so close to home, maybe to be found out by some old acquaintance. As I write this I question myself, what am I to be ashamed of? This is what I was doing in high school. I was clowned plenty in school when I would have a Gideon's New Testament in my back pocket.

I found that character is something that is built over time, and I must remember what character I chose and want to have. While Craig and I were talking, I understood that he was accomplished and a well-known person in the surfing industry. He is one of the heavies and so are his friends. I sensed that Craig was proud and happy with his standing in the surf industry, that is the character that he chose. For Craig to come to terms with himself, saying that he has lost control of his life and had to check into a program, showed me what humbling looks like.

Who in their right mind would want to have to surrender to what has control over them? I know I wouldn't and thank God I did not have to go too. I received mercy with my addiction to alcohol but mine was a different circumstance. Everyone's life is their own to live with free will, that is the gift from our Father above. Our free will and choices always have a way of exposing themselves, in time. As with anyone's life the love from above is the same, but from our point of view it seems to be a different love to others, what we see in our life decisions being exposed the way they do in reality according to our choices that we have made while creating our life pathway.

So it is not fair for us to wish it could be some other way, because it can't be. The truth is that because of our life decisions, that's the way that God's love comes to us. It looks the way it does to an outsider because we all have our own story, a story that we have to own up to. So when we are embraced by the same love from above it only looks the way it does in others because they have made certain choices that God has to deal with in certain ways; it is still the same love of God.

Craig held himself well. I could tell he was trying to hang on to life. The way he told me about the friends he has at the surfboard factory, he tells me that they are pushing for him. Craig thinks that he is going to become a Bible thumper if he goes through The Ranch program. I did not have it in me to say anything about or against that possibility, I just listened. What Craig did tell me is that , the person he works for at that time was in the shop and how he spoke out and asked everyone in the shop if Craig should go to The Ranch? They all said yes!

It was getting late. I could tell that Craig was getting tired of sleeping in the bluffs when he started to ask if he could stay in my van. I put up a wall, I was not going to let him in my van and stay. Is that harsh? So I had nothing else but to put my hand on his shoulder as he was about to walk away and ask God in prayer, with Craig, that He would stay a half of a step in front of us at all times. That seemed to be what Craig held onto for the night. It was hard for me to not let Craig in the van. He asked if he could sleep in the driver's seat. I had to say no. Now how would that look if I park my van, while I'm sleeping in my hammock, hanging in the back, with my dog Eillo on the passenger seat and in the driver's seat would be a drunk stranger! I had to say no, I was reluctant.

The problem I had is that he was still drinking and he asked me to split his last beer, even after I told him I don't drink alcohol any longer. I decided to avoid any possible self-inflicted drama, thinking of a police officer's point of view. So in all well-wishing and encouragement, I asked if he needed a blanket? Craig said yes, and I was happy to let him have a blanket that I had in the van, in case I could share. I think that night he stayed in the campground restroom because Craig told me that he wanted to read the Gospel of John and that he could use the light to see.

I see a bit of myself in most people I meet. I scrutinize myself for some odd reason. At the same time I notice that people will introduce themselves to me, if I make myself available. This is something I am still learning, to be available. My selfish desires take me to places that I am seeing the Lord using to benefit His kingdom. This is beyond me. I just like to go to the popular places. If the Lord feels I am equipped, he brings a new person into my life. I am honored every time the Lord trusts me with a new story of another stranger.

I wonder if the Lord permits His angels to pay special attention to me? Because it feels like I am surrounded by them sometimes. Or if the Lord lets an angel push me in front of the stranger so

He can talk to them. Either way I don't know much about angels but I do know the Bible says there are a lot of them. Or even maybe the stranger is pushed by one... I would like to find out more about how they truly interact with us. I might not know until I get to ask one myself, 'til then I'm keeping a lookout.

I was back on the bluff the next morning. Having a lot of computer work to do, I decided to take a walk first. There is a nice bench that overlooks the bluff. I walked my dog Eillo down there, and checked out the non-existent surf. Kinda glad the surf wasn't inviting, that way I could focus on the work I needed to get done. So back at my desk in my van overlooking the pristine California coast, I sat in my mobile office and took care of my business. As I was finishing up, I felt the need to move the van. I found that I ran my battery down dead.

My van wouldn't start but I was able to run the windows down a bit for some air flow. Shortly after I found this out, now here comes a big Road Ranger RV that decides to back in right next to me. I found this interesting as I was just about the only one in the entire parking lot. The driver walking between my van and his RV exclaims, Home Sweet Home!!

I thought I was done for. I'm
considering calling roadside assistance
before asking my new neighbor for a
jump start. My deadline I was up
against for filing some reports was
already pushing my anxiety up a notch.
It seemed like time was flying as I was
trying to fill out the online forms while
searching out the best data connection
in the area.

More time passed and I wasn't
feeling very social. I decided now was a
good time to see about my solar
powered battery system. I was hoping
to find some long jumper cables so I
could jump start my van from my solar
powered batteries. I knew that I had a
chance because I was successful before,
in Joshua Tree. As I was recollecting
how I was able to charge my dead
battery, I started rummaging in the back
of my van.

Meanwhile my new neighbor is enjoying how loud he can play Led Zeppelin which wasn't totally terrible. I do enjoy a good Zeppelin song once in awhile. This went on for a few songs. I'm noticing that my neighbor had friends showing up to his rig. I thought to myself, this is not how I planned my day to go. A bit of time goes by and I'm watching to see what the next move is going to be but as I got restless, I decided to start tuning up my solar system.

I'm fumbling through my tangled wires and that was when I ended up face to face with my new neighbor introducing himself as Blue. He had a familiar face at first, I was trying to place it. He resembled a good friend from Summit County Colorado. Even stranger was that his friend also resembled another good friend I had in Silverthorne.

I've brushed paths with many people in my life. I'm intrigued how I can be hundreds of miles away from where I previously met a person and even had an ongoing friendship, and then meet a new acquaintance with similarities of another, miles away from each other, now to meet these twins of likeness and mannerisms.

Blue had a sincerity about him which I felt comfortable with. I dropped my protective barrier and let a new friendship begin. I pushed back the urgency of me needing to leave but I still wanted to move. My hotspot Wi-Fi signal was weak. I was still in search of the area that had a strong signal so I could conduct some business online.

I am not sure if I was judging these people that just arrived, but probably was. I didn't know anything except that they moved into my space. I might be a private person. I do like my private space, but I also pray and ask God to bring people into my life. So obviously the prayer gets answered and usually when I don't expect it to be. I forget to always be prepared, and get reminded whenever I miss the easy opportunities and I get frustrated. So God, with His sense of humor, brings some very colorful people into my life, and Yes, answers my prayers.

I feel that there is a purpose for everything with a higher-ordained reason waiting for those that ask for it. To have practice for the kingdom in heaven is what I see when I make contact with other travelers of this world. I am fascinated by the mannerisms of people. As I see reactions, I like to figure out why some of them do what they do. So as I get hung up on me, I am humbled. The stories I hear from these acquaintances amaze me to the extent of being thankful for my life. It could've been different if my dad was not a hard-working man.

My dad made sure his young family were fed, clothed, and housed. What I had to give up of myself when I was growing up was to have a dad that was vacant. Enough about him for he has passed on. I'm just glad that he was a hard-working man to keep his family physically off the streets, but mentally off the street, I'm still not sure. But that's just it, we all have our own story, so I am captivated by the chance of a story of another.

Are we so selfish that we disregard others to a point of, looking away as if unimportant to creating zero interest in even casting your own shadow on the person in despair? Ok, a little off track but I have feelings that drove me to this social experiment I caught myself in the middle of at that moment. I do have interest in why and what makes living on the fringe the option people find themselves in. So there I found myself face to face with a stranger who introduces himself as Blue. I asked him for a jump start. He said, Sure! After some friendly banter and the jump start, I end up moving to a different Wi-Fi spot in the parking lot and Blue went to go get some things to barbeque for his friends.

I did not stick around and try to join in because I was consumed with what I needed to tend to. I'm not sure if at the time when Blue got back he thought it strange that I had moved about 50 yards away. He didn't know it was the Wi-Fi signal strength that caused my need to look for a new location. I was so self-absorbed that I didn't even make an attempt to join in on their barbeque.

So I started in on tuning up my Sprinter's solar power system to start working again. Thinking back that it was a few months since I had them charging my battery system properly so that my computer could work off of it. So after that last time of getting stuck with a dead battery, it prompted me to get my charging system up and running again, like that time in Joshua Tree, the time I had to jump start my van off this solar system. Again I killed my battery by using my computer and listening to the radio, like I repeated to do right then in the San Clemente State Beach lot. That was actually something I figured as a challenge for me to do, a real goal to have the sun power my electronics.

It's the challenge of something that has always grabbed my attention. The pattern I have seen in myself is once I conquer/ figure out/ etcetera I seem to lose interest after the creative part of inventing is over. I lack the follow through. This reminds me of the homeless guy I met outside Norms restaurant one day. I listened to his story about how he hasn't been to the beach since the lifeguards stopped him and told him he needs to wear a bathing suit on the beach. This man I was listening to was surprised that you can't walk on the beach in your underwear...

But that's beside the point I'm getting to. This gentleman did tell me a good line to remember when marketing anything, To not follow up is to foul up. Pretty simple, just wish I could remember that line while the boredom of follow-through starts in. Not sure if it's just me but when the adventure is over I start looking for a new one.

The sad part of realizing this is I missed out on the growth part of relationships. Always looking for the excitement is something I was never shown not to do and the rules of life explained. My bitterness of being under-informed by my parents is now past me. The deal is I have to still figure all this out so I can live in a healthy mindset for the rest of my life. So with that all said, I am starting a new adventure, which I'm doing, writing now.

While I was wrapping up the wires for my solar panels, the sun has been down for maybe an hour. Craig, from the previous night, appeared out of the darkness. He told me that he read the Gospel of John that day. I was impressed, not sure if I ever have done that myself. This is when he told me that he is going to The Ranch in two weeks. I told him that is great to hear. I asked him if he was going to continue drinking 'til he goes? He didn't answer but pondered in his own mind if he was going to. Craig had been drinking already. Again I am reminded of my own drinking style. There was something Craig held onto when we were praying to God together, that was when I asked God to stay a half of a step in front of us at all times.

I believe that our paths orbit around our own being and that others and your own are also pulled together towards the larger orbit, the Spirit of God. While we spin in our own circles we bump into others' circles. At that point, the strength of the magnetism is tested. The polarities of our own inner north and south poles are adjusted. Some circles will not adjust and the magnetic energy repels our orbit and since there is no draw, we continue seeking the source of Life, the Spirit. Still, we go on with our own personal paths. By being aware of this I look for opportunities. I have learned more about myself when I allow my inner balance to be adjusted. My soul is recalibrated. I learn more about my selfish self and focus on the true magnetic source where all power is from, our Creator. This compels me to give and to have compassion for the ones that are one step closer to despair than I am.

The next morning I parked in my new spot where the Wi-Fi was best. It seems to be Bob's favorite spot too. Bob, a new stranger, backed into his spot one space away. He sadly offered me a bag of cat food for Eillo-dog telling me his cat ran away. At the same time, Blue from the day before showed up on a bike and then Donnie and then Johnny showed up. Chris passed by but no sign of Craig. This is my new spot and I'm already packing in a half dozen people talking about how much they are making from canning. This was the start of an interesting turn of events, like a polar shift. I was going out to learn how to earn from recycling cans and bottles for the CRV.

But earlier in the morning I went down to the beach to see if Craig was anywhere visible. We talked the night before about catching waves. I told him how stoked I was on this plastic version of the BodyGlove™ HandGun I picked up at Big 5. I was going body surfing in the morning and I invited him to try one of these Hand planes out, he was in! I saw his bike locked on the rack so I knew he must be somewhere. But time went by and I went back to work at the desk I had set up in my van. Might have missed him while I was at my desk because when I looked for his bike later, it was gone. Still even today at San Clemente State Beach, I have not seen

Craig or his bike since. I hope he made
it to The Ranch.

Part 2

San Clemente is a hard place to get out of… It's more than the waves and the bluffs with beautiful sunsets, it is the aloha feeling. I was in San Clemente's North Side taking care of some business. Parked next to the railroad tracks and looking over the beach with waves crashing on the sand, I was enjoying the beautiful clear day and I fell into a meditative sense. Couldn't help but think about Craig's tragedy as I'm watching the Metrolink train go by with the sun setting over Dana Point's iconic bluff.

I was praying for direction, asking if I should leave. I've been wrestling in my mind about this still, small voice that I have been hearing in my head. And here it is again saying, They need you. Surprised I reply by asking, Huh??? Then the still, small voice responds, You'll see. Now I have heard this voice before and have been wondering about it and its validity. So I figured this would be worth finding out about. The drive south gave my mind time to race with questions of what might be waiting for me back at my favorite area, the bluffs at the State Beach. A barbeque was going on down at the picnic tables. As I was parking I heard my name called out. It was Blue telling me to, Come on down! We have plenty of food! It's Ziggy's birthday!

I greeted Ziggy, wishing him a Happy Birthday! His big sincere smile reminds me of the Cheshire Cat. Ziggy, with a criminal charm, holds himself tall

with pride. Comforting to me seeing
him out of his drug-induced stupor, the
binge aftermath, from the previous
week. Thinking it had been back about
the time we were at the Godalgon
outreach for the second time.
Remembering how the buffet looked
and was delicious! It's so kind of the
people to share their time and food for
the group that flowed past the patio
area, while all listening about God's
love from a local preacher. When I first
met Ziggy he said, I haven't done speed
for 10 days. I said, That's great, thinking
that he was trying to quit. Turns out
that he just hadn't had any money to get
his drugs. So I now had the chance to
get to know Ziggy when he was clear.
He was refreshed looking. He was
eager to tell me where to get free meals
around San Clemente. Ziggy had a plan
for Sundays, telling me to, Always ask
the volunteers serving food for an extra
plate and tell them you are helping out a
friend that couldn't make it. That was

the way Ziggy had been getting by for years. Sure, he did share his food with everyone who asked, but does that justify the subtle lie? I don't have the answer. When a person is hungry, does that change the rules?

I remember we were all enjoying the breakfast buffet. The topic of canning, aka recycling plastic bottles and aluminum cans, came up. After Ziggy and I had our second pass through the buffet, Ziggy's saying, I have an idea for a tee shirt. I said, What's that? And he said, "I live in San Clemente Because I Can." I'm thinking, that seems kind of entitled but he's quick to say, Because I "can," you know, canning! I said, What's canning? And he replied, Canning is when you go get cans and recycle them for the CRV! I go, Wow, you can make money at that? Ziggy said, Maybe enough to feed a chicken! I laughed, listening to Blue and Ziggy tell me stories of how many bags they got from the Surf Competition at Trestles the previous weekend. I figured there was some truth to the story by them proudly wearing the Hurley trucker hats, the kind of swag the crowd gets just by being there. I was stoked for them and feeling envious of the amount of cash they were bragging about. They could tell I wanted to hit that kind of a score. Knowing that surf competition down at Trestles was over and wouldn't be back 'til this time next year, I pry by asking more about how a newbie can be successful at canning.

Blue and Ziggy had caught my interest by bragging on how much money they were making on canning around town. They knew what days to be at the best spots. It seems that canning is a constant way of income. They were leery at first of letting me into their prized territory and sharing their secrets of being a successful canner. My curiosity got me hooked. I had to give it a shot. I had to see if this was a door of opportunity.

Previous to this, I had been working as a Mystery Secret Shopper and have learned how to work for $1 per hour for 15 hours at a time. No joke. So the fact that canning looked more lucrative than working as a spy, I was in! We were off! Blue, Ziggy and me were dreaming of the potential $$$. Ziggy liked to run things and Blue was alright with that, telling me Ziggy should ride shotgun so we can see that he doesn't steal me blind. I grimaced, reminding myself that I have a trust in people. Sure, it has burnt me in the past but I still look for the best in all the people I meet. I whispered a prayer of protection for me and the things in the van as I was promised 5 bucks for gas and elected to be the driver.

From past experience, Blue made it clear that Ziggy was best at digging deep and discerning what was valuable versus garbage as Ziggy started by carefully plucking the recyclables from the depths and tossing them out. Blue and I stood outside the dumpster and packed our bags full while the cans and bottles were flying out from Ziggy's masterful eye. This is what Ziggy has been doing to get by for the past 10 or more years. By the time we were done we must have had a dozen bags of cans and we needed to tie them to the back of my van. So Blue and I went back through the area for a final sweep while the Stand Up Paddleboard event was winding down. While walking back to the parking lot I said to Blue, We are going to need some rope or bungee cords and before I could finish my sentence, all of a sudden out of the tall green grass 3 bungees coiled themselves around my ankles like snakes! Blue said, Why are you surprised? Those bungees were lost there so you would be able to find them when you needed them. I knew he was right but it's something I am learning still, that it can be possible. It reminded me of the time I was surfing up north by Malibu when I needed some sandals to walk on the rocky asphalt after my feet were numbed by the cold water. It was then a pair of sandals appeared as fast as I was thinking of them. It was dark and no one was around, and the sandals were together and pointed in the direction I was walking.

I have recently been meditating on pre-ordained events and situations that angels might have a part in. All of these small, subtle gifts from the unknown come to me as needed when I release my trust to our Creator, of the serendipity and synchronicity, of the ebb and flow of personal life adventures, something I am still learning more of as I allow my curiosity to guide... Anyway, I wish you could have seen all those bags hanging off the back of my Sprinter van. It was a wall of black plastic bags stacked 7' tall! This was a PayDay!

The whole canning experience was a time to bond with two strangers who are now my friends. Even though canning paid better than being a Secret Shopper, the pride of dignity pushed me away from canning. But it is a good option for an emergency.

What I did find out through this is, work is work no matter how far away from it I tempt myself to get. Any way you look at it, work takes effort! All the times I thought it looked easy to be an artist, it got to the point that it took over my life and my ways of discerning reality from what I thought could be real. As I have walked this path, I've seen the beauty of the Creator and I believe that He finds joy in our creativity. So I have sought this creative, roving lifestyle, dreaming of things that I could make come true. What I have gained are many adventures into the unknown levels of humanity, earning my experiences of life and styles of life, from the top to the bottom, in business and in pleasure, all the highs and lows I have survived, giving me a perspective to learn from the challenges of the situations that my decisions bring to me. Everything that I have been able to discover is because of my curiosity, of knowledge becoming wisdom, a young soul becoming an old soul through one's lifetime. I have lived in a surreal/real day-dreaming of an existence most of my life, always looking for an easier way to earn money, fighting off the battle of growing up, while the war of age turns into a grudge of self that wants everything this life offers.

Through my decades of self-indulgence and chasing dreams, I have met many people. Recently I have been pushing through some of my memories. With all of the energy I invested into ways of having the past take care of itself, all the ways I looked to get a clean slate on my memory bank, I still come up empty. The emptiness of the ungratifying "should a would a could a" haunts me still today. The Battle of Right and Wrong is relentless in my mind as my age exceeds what I thought my life would be and brings me to this place I am at now -- a place of grace from above that keeps me from insanity.

I can't visit the past, but my mind can, and will, keep me trapped there if I allow it. The only thing the past is now is a training ground of heart, a place of personal history, a secret place of self. Being there while drifting to the places of "once was" can only be done in one's mind. The danger of that is if I allow it, as my mind ponders the past, then there is where my heart will be also, in the past. This causes division in my life, as if too much dwelling in one place will allow my wheels to rust, slowing my present purpose to a stop while Neil Young has been warning all of us that, "rust never sleeps."

My music collection hasn't been updated much since CDs came out, so while sifting through my old mixed belongings I pick up a dusty cartridge and the tape escaped its place, a loose cassette full of memories now gone. So I wrap the tape around my hand. I have a glimpse of how fleeting a gift of music can be, treasure in the wind only to be trampled as the next best imported goody catches the attention of the masses. Then like a moth drawn to a flame, it will rust and rot turning to dust, tested by fire, burning the dross to

be freed for what goes on and into
forever.

But some in this life strive for more
to have entrusted to them only to find
that it is folly, while others might lie and
cheat a little, all for the greater good. So
I'm not sure about the sincerity of
people and the story that they are
living. What I do know is that
sometimes the people with no worldly
possessions, as simple as it seems, still
have a path and a personalized journey.
That has been where I find God at work,
on the streets with the people that have
a backpack and all that is important
inside it and with them at all times. Or
the people that have ways to hide things
in the shrubs so they can hope that their
belongings are still there when they
return.

Like Johnny who is a Navy
veteran. He had a smile ear to ear and
bright blue eyes. He had a spirit that

glowed, sitting with his backpack with everything he owned in it. Johnny was trying to stay off alcohol. But that was just recently, ever since he had put his trust in Jesus with his own story he is living through. Johnny told me about a time he missed out on some work when he told his possible employer for the day that he needed 5 or 10 minutes to gather his things. Evidently, that was too long to wait for this person and Johnny lost the job. Since then he keeps everything with him always. His backpack is not too big, it looks like the same pack that he kept when he un-listed from the Navy and Johnny is alright with that because his wants are minimal. Johnny has kids who love and accept where he's at, and Johnny's made peace with his kids. Seems to be a reverse form of tough love, not an easy emotion but any kind of love is tough.

The next night the sun was setting while Blue, Johnny and Ziggy started up a bonfire rekindled from the night before, the same wood was still smoldering from the one they had for Ziggy's birthday. We were standing close to the fire ring talking about the stars and planets. God was keeping me in San Clemente longer than I had planned. I constantly was praying to have His guidance and all I heard was, You'll see. And out from the darkness of the night I saw Craig walking up to the bonfire. He said that he made it in hopes of running into me. And that phrase from the small, soft voice, You'll see, left after I ran into Craig at the bluffs.

I've been wondering about him even to the point of going to the surf shop where Craig said he did most of his board glassing art work. We all chatted for awhile and then humbly the first thing he had to share was his news of going to that sober camp for 30 days, the one that the pastor had set up for him. Surprised me so I asked when? Turns out he was going the next morning. His brother was on board to give him the ride he needed. Craig already knew most of the people around the fire ring. The vibe around the pit was warm and all of the faces staring at the flames, so when Craig said about how he was going to the recovery ranch the next day, it caught everyone by surprise! The mood changed a bit. I'm guessing that it caused all the others to think about themselves for a moment.

Craig didn't know that when I asked where it was, it was because I was encouraged by my family to go out there for my own alcoholic spiritual battle. I kept it to myself because I was still in denial that a place like The Ranch would have worked out for myself.

I have also had dreams in the past of things before they happen, giving me a surreal sensation. I had heard on the AM radio about a woman dying on the railroad tracks in San Clemente. It was only a short news blast and I never heard more about her. That was a few months before meeting Craig; turns out that woman was his wife, who tore his heart and soul out when she stepped into the railroad tracks. That moment at the firepit, I made the connection and felt flush in awe that I was standing face to face with the person who was on the opposite end of that news blast. I was stuck like a deer in headlights. I was searching my mind for the source of this new sensation. Honestly I have never known that there's a different word than sympathy, being empathy. I was learning in this certain moment. I thought about how bad someone would have to feel to do that. That's what had driven Craig to the bottle, out of his despair. Craig didn't know that I knew this story. I'm not even sure how I heard a quiet news blast about a woman that took her own life on the railroad tracks in front of the bluffs in San Clemente. The same bluffs that Craig recently has been sleeping in.

It was getting late and the temperature was dropping. It was time to go and Craig knew it. I gave him a ride across town. It helped my soul feel settled to see there was someone else at the church parking lot getting some things together and preparing for the cold night. Turns out this person had recently run a sober living house and had to close it down because of some city ordinances and was now homeless himself. Here I was, able to see that God was working by helping Craig out and getting him ready to make his complete surrender, to allow the Spirit of God to fight his battle against the spirit of alcohol.

The best I could do was give him a jacket that I had with me. Craig was thankful for that and for the ride and said he didn't mind sleeping at the church for the night. When I pulled away I had to fight off the feeling of needing to do more. But I reminded myself that I am only one part of the complete body of humanity. I did my part, plus the gentleman that was there seemed to be expecting Craig to show up that night at the church parking lot.

Driving back to the San Clemente bluffs I felt at peace. I have met many people in San Clemente. There are some that have the Lord in their hearts, and some that are wondering about what the Lord is.

When Blue told me the way he felt about my dog Eillo, Blue seemed to want to hold it to himself but I am glad he didn't. When he said that there is no denying that there is a living, loving God when he sees the unconditional love that my dog Eillo has for everyone,

Blue said that proves there is a Creator.

It made me sad when he told me why he thinks he turned out the way he did. It was when he got this mini bike as a kid and that was all he could think of. His dad asked him to mow the yard after school and Blue was obsessed with this mini bike and he finally got it running good. All he could do was get on that mini bike after school, forgetting to mow the lawn. Blue said it hurt so much when he came home after school the next day to find his mini bike cut up into pieces.

It took awhile to understand the depth of the harm that it did to my friend Blue. I needed to hear his story; it took me awhile to realize it and why it stuck in my mind. My dad did similar detrimental actions towards me. My dad was a shining star when he was out and away from his family; he had a drive that he couldn't leave at the office.

So us, the family, got the brunt of the frustrations of a vacant but present father.

With my history of anxiety I feared that I would be feeling the guilt of passing on a curse to my next generation so, honestly, looking back at my life, knowing now that I had a generational curse to break, this situation Blue went through was reminding me of my deciding point. I never imagined I was going to see it constructed in another person's life, bringing back a memory that formed a dichotomy I hid away. Not sure if I am ready to share more thoughts about what caused my division between my father and me, just humbling to observe and ponder in another person's life. So while I have not been able to purge myself of the pain from my selfish living, what I do have is a sense of freedom when I trust the Spirit of God to guide.

This brings me back to my memories of Santa Monica and the drive that brought me there when I made my first attempt to break free from the Inland Empire, a few years previous to all this. It was then that I discovered when I listen to the people that have stories of their lives to share with me, there is one thing I find in common, the same thing I fear, the fact of the past and how it tries to control the future. Whispering to myself, Don't be robbed of time, it is better to release. But as I write these words I ask God for the ability to do just that, one moment at a time. I have noticed that if I pay attention to some of the stories I am told, I can gain guidance for similar situations I might come across. The test is, if I can keep myself out of the way of the Spirit, I find it leads to a new place, a plateau that gives me a view of the world in a way I have not seen before, inspiring a desire to know God in a closer way, to the level that was put on my path, to learn from the life I have dismantled by living through my selfish desires, only able to achieve daily life by my surrendering to the Higher Power that has become my strength in hope to become the better man.

About the Author

Not long ago, Roger Cerny took himself off the grid to conduct a self-described "sociology experiment". Born from an innate curiosity and a belief that everyone has a story to tell, Roger traveled throughout Southern California in his Sprinter Van spending time with people living on the fringes of society, listening to their stories. After his second cancer surgery, Roger put the van aside and started traveling in an RV. Honoring a promise he made with God, these roving yarns give a voice to the ones he met, and remind us that we are all a part of One Humanity, no matter what path each of us is on.

Born and raised in Orange County, California, Roger ran his own door contracting company at age 20 until the lure of the mountains and snow in Colorado promised more months of snowboarding. Living in Breckenridge, he was introduced to photography and Summit snowboards and made longboard-skateboards. After moving back to Orange County, Roger created WaveGuns™, designing the first unique, concave wooden bodysurfing hand plane, landing them in surf shops from San Diego to Santa Barbara.

www.ingramcontent.com/pod-product-compliance
Lightning Source LLC
Chambersburg PA
CBHW040232240726
48664CB00001B/97